The GOLFER'S LOG BOOK

THE NEW
ZEROLENE
"WINS-all the way!"

A BULFINCH PRESS BOOK

Little, Brown and Company • Boston, Toronto, London

COPYRIGHTS

Cover:
Golf. Lepas.
Collection of Sarah Fabian Baddiel, London.

Title page:
Zerolene. Artist unknown.
Wood River Gallery.

Contents page:
Donald Duck.
Collection of Sarah Fabian Baddiel, London.

First Edition

ISBN 0-8212-1966-9

Bulfinch Press is an imprint and trademark of
Little, Brown and Company (Inc.)

Published simultaneously in Canada by
Little, Brown & Company (Canada) Limited

PRINTED IN SINGAPORE

CONTENTS

ROUNDS PLAYED   4

GOLF COURSES   84

GOLF PARTNERS   94

GOLF GAMES   108

ROUNDS PLAYED

GOLF COURSE _____ DATE _____

PAR _____ YARDAGE _____

SELF _____ SCORE _____ HANDICAP _____

PARTNER 1 _____ SCORE _____ HANDICAP _____

PARTNER 2 _____ SCORE _____ HANDICAP _____

PARTNER 3 _____ SCORE _____ HANDICAP _____

COMMENTS _____

_____

_____

GOLF COURSE _____ DATE _____

PAR _____ YARDAGE _____

SELF _____ SCORE _____ HANDICAP _____

PARTNER 1 _____ SCORE _____ HANDICAP _____

PARTNER 2 _____ SCORE _____ HANDICAP _____

PARTNER 3 _____ SCORE _____ HANDICAP _____

COMMENTS _____

_____

_____

Harper's. April 1898. Artist unknown.
Wood River Gallery.

5

ROUNDS PLAYED

GOLF COURSE _____   DATE _____

PAR _____   YARDAGE _____

SELF _____   SCORE _____   HANDICAP _____

PARTNER 1 _____   SCORE _____   HANDICAP _____

PARTNER 2 _____   SCORE _____   HANDICAP _____

PARTNER 3 _____   SCORE _____   HANDICAP _____

COMMENTS _____

_____

_____

GOLF COURSE _____   DATE _____

PAR _____   YARDAGE _____

SELF _____   SCORE _____   HANDICAP _____

PARTNER 1 _____   SCORE _____   HANDICAP _____

PARTNER 2 _____   SCORE _____   HANDICAP _____

PARTNER 3 _____   SCORE _____   HANDICAP _____

COMMENTS _____

_____

_____

6

Outing. Artist unknown.
Collection of Karen and Ralph Elder.

Outing

HARPER'S WEEKLY

EDITED BY

GEORGE HARVEY

"Come one, come all! this rock shall fly
From its firm base as soon as I."

August 31 1912   HARPER & BROTHERS, N. Y.   Price 10 Cents

ROUNDS PLAYED

GOLF COURSE

DATE

PAR

YARDAGE

SELF

SCORE   HANDICAP

PARTNER 1

SCORE   HANDICAP

PARTNER 2

SCORE   HANDICAP

PARTNER 3

SCORE   HANDICAP

COMMENTS

GOLF COURSE

DATE

PAR

YARDAGE

SELF

SCORE   HANDICAP

PARTNER 1

SCORE   HANDICAP

PARTNER 2

SCORE   HANDICAP

PARTNER 3

SCORE   HANDICAP

COMMENTS

Harper's Weekly [President William Taft].
August 31, 1912.
C. F. Budd. Wood River Gallery.

9

ROUNDS PLAYED

GOLF COURSE

DATE

PAR

YARDAGE

SELF

SCORE   HANDICAP

PARTNER 1

SCORE   HANDICAP

PARTNER 2

SCORE   HANDICAP

PARTNER 3

SCORE   HANDICAP

COMMENTS

GOLF COURSE

DATE

PAR

YARDAGE

SELF

SCORE   HANDICAP

PARTNER 1

SCORE   HANDICAP

PARTNER 2

SCORE   HANDICAP

PARTNER 3

SCORE   HANDICAP

COMMENTS

10

Crawford's Assorted Scotch Shortbread.
1928. Artist unknown.
Collection of Karen and Ralph Elder.

By Appointment

"Leading"

CRAWFORD'S
ASSORTED
SCOTCH SHORTBREAD
THE SHORTBREAD OF TRADITION.
Delightful for Afternoon Tea and Social Functions.

ROUNDS PLAYED

●

GOLF COURSE _____ DATE _____

PAR _____ YARDAGE _____

SELF _____ SCORE _____ HANDICAP _____

PARTNER 1 _____ SCORE _____ HANDICAP _____

PARTNER 2 _____ SCORE _____ HANDICAP _____

PARTNER 3 _____ SCORE _____ HANDICAP _____

COMMENTS _____

_____

_____

GOLF COURSE _____ DATE _____

PAR _____ YARDAGE _____

SELF _____ SCORE _____ HANDICAP _____

PARTNER 1 _____ SCORE _____ HANDICAP _____

PARTNER 2 _____ SCORE _____ HANDICAP _____

PARTNER 3 _____ SCORE _____ HANDICAP _____

COMMENTS _____

_____

_____

13
●

ROUNDS PLAYED

●

GOLF COURSE _____ DATE _____

PAR _____ YARDAGE _____

SELF _____ SCORE _____ HANDICAP _____

PARTNER 1 _____ SCORE _____ HANDICAP _____

PARTNER 2 _____ SCORE _____ HANDICAP _____

PARTNER 3 _____ SCORE _____ HANDICAP _____

COMMENTS _____

_____

_____

GOLF COURSE _____ DATE _____

PAR _____ YARDAGE _____

SELF _____ SCORE _____ HANDICAP _____

PARTNER 1 _____ SCORE _____ HANDICAP _____

PARTNER 2 _____ SCORE _____ HANDICAP _____

PARTNER 3 _____ SCORE _____ HANDICAP _____

COMMENTS _____

_____

_____

●

Harper's Round Table Christmas.
Maxfield Parrish.
Collection of Karen and Ralph Elder.

HARPER'S
ROVND TABLE

CHRISTMAS

ROUNDS PLAYED

GOLF COURSE

DATE

PAR

YARDAGE

SELF

SCORE   HANDICAP

PARTNER 1

SCORE   HANDICAP

PARTNER 2

SCORE   HANDICAP

PARTNER 3

SCORE   HANDICAP

COMMENTS

GOLF COURSE

DATE

PAR

YARDAGE

SELF

SCORE   HANDICAP

PARTNER 1

SCORE   HANDICAP

PARTNER 2

SCORE   HANDICAP

PARTNER 3

SCORE   HANDICAP

COMMENTS

Great Eastern Railway. Circa 1920.
John Hassall. Wood River Gallery.

17

ROUNDS PLAYED

GOLF COURSE

DATE

PAR

YARDAGE

SELF

SCORE   HANDICAP

PARTNER 1

SCORE   HANDICAP

PARTNER 2

SCORE   HANDICAP

PARTNER 3

SCORE   HANDICAP

COMMENTS

GOLF COURSE

DATE

PAR

YARDAGE

SELF

SCORE   HANDICAP

PARTNER 1

SCORE   HANDICAP

PARTNER 2

SCORE   HANDICAP

PARTNER 3

SCORE   HANDICAP

COMMENTS

18

La Cañada Fruit Growers' Association.
Artist unknown. Wood River Gallery.

BY WILMOT LUNT   THE GOLF GIRL

ROUNDS PLAYED

GOLF COURSE _____

DATE _____

PAR _____

YARDAGE _____

SELF _____ SCORE _____ HANDICAP _____

PARTNER 1 _____ SCORE _____ HANDICAP _____

PARTNER 2 _____ SCORE _____ HANDICAP _____

PARTNER 3 _____ SCORE _____ HANDICAP _____

COMMENTS _____

_____

_____

GOLF COURSE _____

DATE _____

PAR _____

YARDAGE _____

SELF _____ SCORE _____ HANDICAP _____

PARTNER 1 _____ SCORE _____ HANDICAP _____

PARTNER 2 _____ SCORE _____ HANDICAP _____

PARTNER 3 _____ SCORE _____ HANDICAP _____

COMMENTS _____

_____

_____

The Golf Girl. Wilmot Lunt.
Collection of Karen and Ralph Elder.

ROUNDS PLAYED

●

GOLF COURSE _____ DATE _____

PAR _____ YARDAGE _____

SELF _____ SCORE _____ HANDICAP _____

PARTNER 1 _____ SCORE _____ HANDICAP _____

PARTNER 2 _____ SCORE _____ HANDICAP _____

PARTNER 3 _____ SCORE _____ HANDICAP _____

COMMENTS _____

_____

_____

GOLF COURSE _____ DATE _____

PAR _____ YARDAGE _____

SELF _____ SCORE _____ HANDICAP _____

PARTNER 1 _____ SCORE _____ HANDICAP _____

PARTNER 2 _____ SCORE _____ HANDICAP _____

PARTNER 3 _____ SCORE _____ HANDICAP _____

COMMENTS _____

_____

_____

●

The Ford Motor Company. 1930.
Artist unknown. Wood River Gallery.

An admired grace of line and contour

SEEING the new Ford as it speeds along the broad highway or parked proudly beside the cool green of the Country Club, you are impressed by its flowing grace of line and contour. There is about it, in appearance and performance, a substantial excellence which sets it apart and gives it character and position unusual in a low-priced car. To women especially, its safety, its comfort, its reliability and its surprising ease of operation and control have put a new joy in motoring. « « « « « « « «

THE NEW FORD COUPE

60ᵉ Année. N° 38 — Le Numéro : 1 fr. 50 — Samedi 23 Septembre 1922

LA VIE PARISIENNE

Rédaction, Administration & Publicité : 10, rue Tronchet, Paris.

ROUNDS PLAYED

GOLF COURSE

DATE

PAR

YARDAGE

SELF

SCORE   HANDICAP

PARTNER 1

SCORE   HANDICAP

PARTNER 2

SCORE   HANDICAP

PARTNER 3

SCORE   HANDICAP

COMMENTS

GOLF COURSE

DATE

PAR

YARDAGE

SELF

SCORE   HANDICAP

PARTNER 1

SCORE   HANDICAP

PARTNER 2

SCORE   HANDICAP

PARTNER 3

SCORE   HANDICAP

COMMENTS

La Vie Parisienne. September 23, 1922.
Herouard. Wood River Gallery.

25

ROUNDS PLAYED

GOLF COURSE _____ DATE _____

PAR _____ YARDAGE _____

SELF _____ SCORE _____ HANDICAP _____

PARTNER 1 _____ SCORE _____ HANDICAP _____

PARTNER 2 _____ SCORE _____ HANDICAP _____

PARTNER 3 _____ SCORE _____ HANDICAP _____

COMMENTS _____

GOLF COURSE _____ DATE _____

PAR _____ YARDAGE _____

SELF _____ SCORE _____ HANDICAP _____

PARTNER 1 _____ SCORE _____ HANDICAP _____

PARTNER 2 _____ SCORE _____ HANDICAP _____

PARTNER 3 _____ SCORE _____ HANDICAP _____

COMMENTS _____

26

Interwoven Toe and Heel Socks.
Norman Rockwell.
Collection of Karen and Ralph Elder.

Interwoven
Toe and Heel
Socks

A LONG WAY TO THE FIRST HOLE

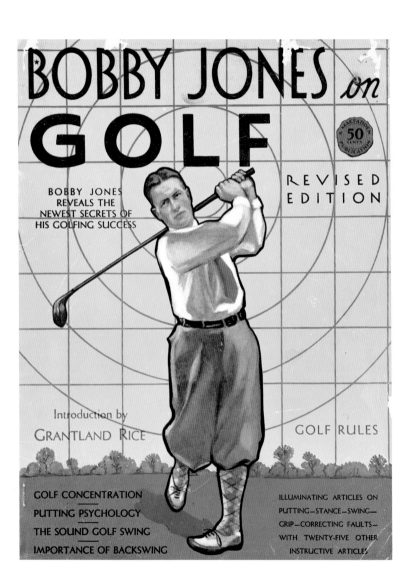

BOBBY JONES *on*
GOLF

A MACFADDEN PUBLICATION · 50 CENTS

BOBBY JONES
REVEALS THE
NEWEST SECRETS OF
HIS GOLFING SUCCESS

REVISED
EDITION

Introduction by
GRANTLAND RICE

GOLF RULES

GOLF CONCENTRATION

PUTTING PSYCHOLOGY

THE SOUND GOLF SWING

IMPORTANCE OF BACKSWING

ILLUMINATING ARTICLES ON
PUTTING—STANCE—SWING—
GRIP—CORRECTING FAULTS—
WITH TWENTY-FIVE OTHER
INSTRUCTIVE ARTICLES

ROUNDS PLAYED

●

GOLF COURSE _____ DATE _____

PAR _____ YARDAGE _____

SELF _____ SCORE _____ HANDICAP _____

PARTNER 1 _____ SCORE _____ HANDICAP _____

PARTNER 2 _____ SCORE _____ HANDICAP _____

PARTNER 3 _____ SCORE _____ HANDICAP _____

COMMENTS _____

_____

_____

GOLF COURSE _____ DATE _____

PAR _____ YARDAGE _____

SELF _____ SCORE _____ HANDICAP _____

PARTNER 1 _____ SCORE _____ HANDICAP _____

PARTNER 2 _____ SCORE _____ HANDICAP _____

PARTNER 3 _____ SCORE _____ HANDICAP _____

COMMENTS _____

_____

_____

Bobby Jones on Golf, revised edition.
Artist unknown. Collection of
Sarah Fabian Baddiel, London.

29

●

ROUNDS PLAYED

●

GOLF COURSE _____ DATE _____

PAR _____ YARDAGE _____

SELF _____ SCORE _____ HANDICAP _____

PARTNER 1 _____ SCORE _____ HANDICAP _____

PARTNER 2 _____ SCORE _____ HANDICAP _____

PARTNER 3 _____ SCORE _____ HANDICAP _____

COMMENTS _____

_____

_____

GOLF COURSE _____ DATE _____

PAR _____ YARDAGE _____

SELF _____ SCORE _____ HANDICAP _____

PARTNER 1 _____ SCORE _____ HANDICAP _____

PARTNER 2 _____ SCORE _____ HANDICAP _____

PARTNER 3 _____ SCORE _____ HANDICAP _____

COMMENTS _____

_____

_____

30

●

The Golf Girl. Circa 1900. Rob Wagner.
Courtesy of Kennedy Galleries, Inc.,
New York. Photo courtesy of Sally Fox,
The Picture Company.

THE GOLF GIRL

ROUNDS PLAYED

GOLF COURSE _____ DATE _____

PAR _____ YARDAGE _____

SELF _____ SCORE _____ HANDICAP _____

PARTNER 1 _____ SCORE _____ HANDICAP _____

PARTNER 2 _____ SCORE _____ HANDICAP _____

PARTNER 3 _____ SCORE _____ HANDICAP _____

COMMENTS _____

GOLF COURSE _____ DATE _____

PAR _____ YARDAGE _____

SELF _____ SCORE _____ HANDICAP _____

PARTNER 1 _____ SCORE _____ HANDICAP _____

PARTNER 2 _____ SCORE _____ HANDICAP _____

PARTNER 3 _____ SCORE _____ HANDICAP _____

COMMENTS _____

Golf. A. Meiresonne. Collection of
Sarah Fabian Baddiel, London.

33

ROUNDS PLAYED

GOLF COURSE _____ DATE _____

PAR _____ YARDAGE _____

SELF _____ SCORE _____ HANDICAP _____

PARTNER 1 _____ SCORE _____ HANDICAP _____

PARTNER 2 _____ SCORE _____ HANDICAP _____

PARTNER 3 _____ SCORE _____ HANDICAP _____

COMMENTS _____

_____

_____

GOLF COURSE _____ DATE _____

PAR _____ YARDAGE _____

SELF _____ SCORE _____ HANDICAP _____

PARTNER 1 _____ SCORE _____ HANDICAP _____

PARTNER 2 _____ SCORE _____ HANDICAP _____

PARTNER 3 _____ SCORE _____ HANDICAP _____

COMMENTS _____

_____

_____

Artist unknown. Collection of Sarah
Fabian Baddiel, London.

ROUNDS PLAYED

●

GOLF COURSE _____ DATE _____

PAR _____ YARDAGE _____

SELF _____ SCORE _____ HANDICAP _____

PARTNER 1 _____ SCORE _____ HANDICAP _____

PARTNER 2 _____ SCORE _____ HANDICAP _____

PARTNER 3 _____ SCORE _____ HANDICAP _____

COMMENTS _____

_____

_____

GOLF COURSE _____ DATE _____

PAR _____ YARDAGE _____

SELF _____ SCORE _____ HANDICAP _____

PARTNER 1 _____ SCORE _____ HANDICAP _____

PARTNER 2 _____ SCORE _____ HANDICAP _____

PARTNER 3 _____ SCORE _____ HANDICAP _____

COMMENTS _____

_____

_____

365. Reg Carter. Collection of Sarah
Fabian Baddiel, London.

●

ROUNDS PLAYED

●

GOLF COURSE _____ DATE _____

PAR _____ YARDAGE _____

SELF _____ SCORE _____ HANDICAP _____

PARTNER 1 _____ SCORE _____ HANDICAP _____

PARTNER 2 _____ SCORE _____ HANDICAP _____

PARTNER 3 _____ SCORE _____ HANDICAP _____

COMMENTS _____

_____

_____

GOLF COURSE _____ DATE _____

PAR _____ YARDAGE _____

SELF _____ SCORE _____ HANDICAP _____

PARTNER 1 _____ SCORE _____ HANDICAP _____

PARTNER 2 _____ SCORE _____ HANDICAP _____

PARTNER 3 _____ SCORE _____ HANDICAP _____

COMMENTS _____

_____

_____

●

The Caddy. Fred T. Ashton. Collection of Sarah Fabian Baddiel, London.

Beginning THE MAN WHO SAVED THE WORLD
By E. Phillips Oppenheim

August 18, 1934

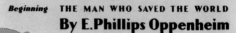

5¢ a copy
10c in Canada

Collier's
THE NATIONAL WEEKLY

**More
than
2,250,000
Circulation**

arthur
crouch,

ROUNDS PLAYED

●

GOLF COURSE _____

DATE _____

PAR _____

YARDAGE _____

SELF _____

SCORE _____ HANDICAP _____

PARTNER 1 _____

SCORE _____ HANDICAP _____

PARTNER 2 _____

SCORE _____ HANDICAP _____

PARTNER 3 _____

SCORE _____ HANDICAP _____

COMMENTS _____

_____

_____

GOLF COURSE _____

DATE _____

PAR _____

YARDAGE _____

SELF _____

SCORE _____ HANDICAP _____

PARTNER 1 _____

SCORE _____ HANDICAP _____

PARTNER 2 _____

SCORE _____ HANDICAP _____

PARTNER 3 _____

SCORE _____ HANDICAP _____

COMMENTS _____

_____

_____

Collier's. August 18, 1934.
Arthur Crouch. Wood River Gallery.

41
●

ROUNDS PLAYED

GOLF COURSE

DATE

PAR

YARDAGE

SELF

SCORE

HANDICAP

PARTNER 1

SCORE

HANDICAP

PARTNER 2

SCORE

HANDICAP

PARTNER 3

SCORE

HANDICAP

COMMENTS

GOLF COURSE

DATE

PAR

YARDAGE

SELF

SCORE

HANDICAP

PARTNER 1

SCORE

HANDICAP

PARTNER 2

SCORE

HANDICAP

PARTNER 3

SCORE

HANDICAP

COMMENTS

Bradley Knitting Company.
Artist unknown. Wood River Gallery.

OPINIONS may vary as to whether the gentleman's *stance* is correct. But one thing is certain. He is *dressed* exactly right. For he is wearing one of the new Bradley golf combinations—a knitted pullover sweater and stockings to match.

One is certain to find himself frequently in the presence of these unusually effective, matched outfits this season. Quite as often, perhaps, as though he played the fashionable courses at Gleneagles or St. Andrews.

Your Bradley dealer is now showing the smart Bradley golf combinations with matching stockings. He offers them with pull-over, straight buttoned jackets or buttoned blouses. The colors range from the most inconspicuous shades to the gayest of Glasgow plaids. Try them on. See what a difference they make.

Note particularly the trim, comfortable fit, the sturdy elastic knitting, the reasonable prices—$12 to $20 per set. These are advantages always found in every Bradley-knit garment. Above all else, look for the Bradley label. For 20 years this famous label has been an unfailing index to satisfaction and genuine economy in all types of knitted outerwear.

*   *   *

Copies of Bradley's booklets "Spring and Summer Styles" and "How to Swim" will be sent to any address, postpaid, upon request.

BRADLEY   KNITTING   COMPANY,   DELAVAN,   WIS.

Golf Number

Life

Price 15 Cents

October 14, 1920

Vol. 76. Copyright, 1920, Life Publishing Company. No. 1980

"Fore!"

ROUNDS PLAYED

●

GOLF COURSE _____   DATE _____

PAR _____   YARDAGE _____

SELF _____   SCORE _____   HANDICAP _____

PARTNER 1 _____   SCORE _____   HANDICAP _____

PARTNER 2 _____   SCORE _____   HANDICAP _____

PARTNER 3 _____   SCORE _____   HANDICAP _____

COMMENTS _____

_____

_____

GOLF COURSE _____   DATE _____

PAR _____   YARDAGE _____

SELF _____   SCORE _____   HANDICAP _____

PARTNER 1 _____   SCORE _____   HANDICAP _____

PARTNER 2 _____   SCORE _____   HANDICAP _____

PARTNER 3 _____   SCORE _____   HANDICAP _____

COMMENTS _____

_____

_____

Life. October 14, 1920. Coles Phillips.
Wood River Gallery.

45

●

ROUNDS PLAYED

●

GOLF COURSE   DATE

PAR   YARDAGE

SELF   SCORE   HANDICAP

PARTNER 1   SCORE   HANDICAP

PARTNER 2   SCORE   HANDICAP

PARTNER 3   SCORE   HANDICAP

COMMENTS

GOLF COURSE   DATE

PAR   YARDAGE

SELF   SCORE   HANDICAP

PARTNER 1   SCORE   HANDICAP

PARTNER 2   SCORE   HANDICAP

PARTNER 3   SCORE   HANDICAP

COMMENTS

●

Life. May 8, 1931. Ed Graham.
Collection of Karen and Ralph Elder.

WEEK
ENDING
SEPT. 27
1924

5¢

Liberty

A Weekly for Everybody

"The Wearing of the Green"

JOSEPH
FARRELLY

In this Issue: **WINNERS** *in the* **COMPOSITE DOG CONTEST**

ROUNDS PLAYED

●

GOLF COURSE _____ DATE _____

PAR _____ YARDAGE _____

SELF _____ SCORE _____ HANDICAP _____

PARTNER 1 _____ SCORE _____ HANDICAP _____

PARTNER 2 _____ SCORE _____ HANDICAP _____

PARTNER 3 _____ SCORE _____ HANDICAP _____

COMMENTS _____

GOLF COURSE _____ DATE _____

PAR _____ YARDAGE _____

SELF _____ SCORE _____ HANDICAP _____

PARTNER 1 _____ SCORE _____ HANDICAP _____

PARTNER 2 _____ SCORE _____ HANDICAP _____

PARTNER 3 _____ SCORE _____ HANDICAP _____

COMMENTS _____

Liberty. September 27, 1924.
Joseph Farrelly.
Collection of Karen and Ralph Elder.

●

ROUNDS PLAYED

●

GOLF COURSE _____ DATE _____

PAR _____ YARDAGE _____

SELF _____ SCORE _____ HANDICAP _____

PARTNER 1 _____ SCORE _____ HANDICAP _____

PARTNER 2 _____ SCORE _____ HANDICAP _____

PARTNER 3 _____ SCORE _____ HANDICAP _____

COMMENTS _____

_____

_____

GOLF COURSE _____ DATE _____

PAR _____ YARDAGE _____

SELF _____ SCORE _____ HANDICAP _____

PARTNER 1 _____ SCORE _____ HANDICAP _____

PARTNER 2 _____ SCORE _____ HANDICAP _____

PARTNER 3 _____ SCORE _____ HANDICAP _____

COMMENTS _____

_____

_____

50

Dunlop Figurine. Artist unknown.
Collection of Sarah Fabian Baddiel,
London.

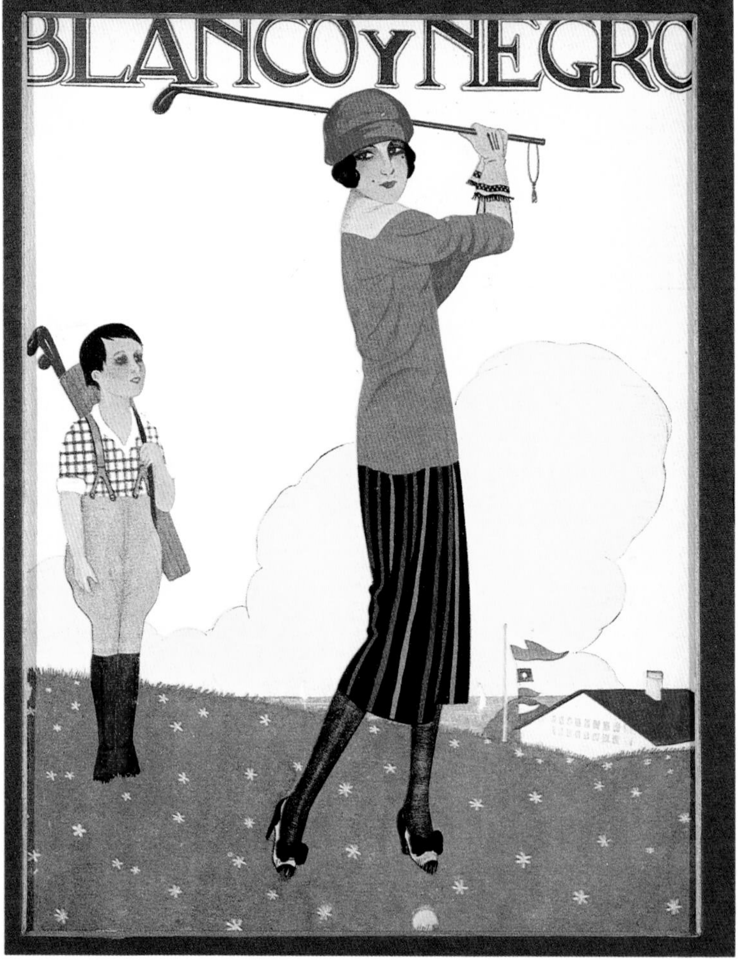
BLANCO Y NEGRO

ROUNDS PLAYED

●

GOLF COURSE _____ DATE _____

PAR _____ YARDAGE _____

SELF _____ SCORE _____ HANDICAP _____

PARTNER 1 _____ SCORE _____ HANDICAP _____

PARTNER 2 _____ SCORE _____ HANDICAP _____

PARTNER 3 _____ SCORE _____ HANDICAP _____

COMMENTS _____

_____

_____

GOLF COURSE _____ DATE _____

PAR _____ YARDAGE _____

SELF _____ SCORE _____ HANDICAP _____

PARTNER 1 _____ SCORE _____ HANDICAP _____

PARTNER 2 _____ SCORE _____ HANDICAP _____

PARTNER 3 _____ SCORE _____ HANDICAP _____

COMMENTS _____

_____

_____

Blanco y Negro. Artist unknown.
Collection of Sarah Fabian Baddiel,
London.

53

●

ROUNDS PLAYED

●

GOLF COURSE _____   DATE _____

PAR _____   YARDAGE _____

SELF _____   SCORE _____   HANDICAP _____

PARTNER 1 _____   SCORE _____   HANDICAP _____

PARTNER 2 _____   SCORE _____   HANDICAP _____

PARTNER 3 _____   SCORE _____   HANDICAP _____

COMMENTS _____

_____

_____

GOLF COURSE _____   DATE _____

PAR _____   YARDAGE _____

SELF _____   SCORE _____   HANDICAP _____

PARTNER 1 _____   SCORE _____   HANDICAP _____

PARTNER 2 _____   SCORE _____   HANDICAP _____

PARTNER 3 _____   SCORE _____   HANDICAP _____

COMMENTS _____

_____

_____

●

Le Sourire. Aquarelle de Jaquelux.
Collection of Sarah Fabian Baddiel,
London.

28ᵉ Année. Nᵒ 410   Prix : 1 Fr. 50   JEUDI 12 MARS 1925

le Sourire

GOLF

Il n'arrive jamais à mettre dans le trou.

Aquarelle de Jaquelux

INN DIXIE

JUNE, 1935   VOL. 2   NO. 6

A MONTHLY MAGAZINE FOR GUESTS OF DINKLER HOTELS

ROUNDS PLAYED

●

GOLF COURSE _____ DATE _____

PAR _____ YARDAGE _____

SELF _____ SCORE _____ HANDICAP _____

PARTNER 1 _____ SCORE _____ HANDICAP _____

PARTNER 2 _____ SCORE _____ HANDICAP _____

PARTNER 3 _____ SCORE _____ HANDICAP _____

COMMENTS _____

_____

_____

GOLF COURSE _____ DATE _____

PAR _____ YARDAGE _____

SELF _____ SCORE _____ HANDICAP _____

PARTNER 1 _____ SCORE _____ HANDICAP _____

PARTNER 2 _____ SCORE _____ HANDICAP _____

PARTNER 3 _____ SCORE _____ HANDICAP _____

COMMENTS _____

_____

_____

Inn Dixie. June 1935. Artist unknown.
Wood River Gallery.

●

ROUNDS PLAYED

●

GOLF COURSE _____   DATE _____

PAR _____   YARDAGE _____

SELF _____   SCORE _____   HANDICAP _____

PARTNER 1 _____   SCORE _____   HANDICAP _____

PARTNER 2 _____   SCORE _____   HANDICAP _____

PARTNER 3 _____   SCORE _____   HANDICAP _____

COMMENTS _____
_____
_____

GOLF COURSE _____   DATE _____

PAR _____   YARDAGE _____

SELF _____   SCORE _____   HANDICAP _____

PARTNER 1 _____   SCORE _____   HANDICAP _____

PARTNER 2 _____   SCORE _____   HANDICAP _____

PARTNER 3 _____   SCORE _____   HANDICAP _____

COMMENTS _____
_____
_____

58
●

Sports d'Été et d'Hiver
Station d'altitude 1550 m. (5000 Feet)

MONTANA–VERMALA
s/SIERRE (SUISSE)

ROUNDS PLAYED

●

GOLF COURSE _____ DATE _____

PAR _____ YARDAGE _____

SELF _____ SCORE _____ HANDICAP _____

PARTNER 1 _____ SCORE _____ HANDICAP _____

PARTNER 2 _____ SCORE _____ HANDICAP _____

PARTNER 3 _____ SCORE _____ HANDICAP _____

COMMENTS _____

_____

_____

GOLF COURSE _____ DATE _____

PAR _____ YARDAGE _____

SELF _____ SCORE _____ HANDICAP _____

PARTNER 1 _____ SCORE _____ HANDICAP _____

PARTNER 2 _____ SCORE _____ HANDICAP _____

PARTNER 3 _____ SCORE _____ HANDICAP _____

COMMENTS _____

_____

_____

Montana-Vermala travel poster.
Circa 1930. Artist unknown.
Wood River Gallery.

61

ROUNDS PLAYED

●

GOLF COURSE _____ DATE _____

PAR _____ YARDAGE _____

SELF _____ SCORE _____ HANDICAP _____

PARTNER 1 _____ SCORE _____ HANDICAP _____

PARTNER 2 _____ SCORE _____ HANDICAP _____

PARTNER 3 _____ SCORE _____ HANDICAP _____

COMMENTS _____

_____

_____

GOLF COURSE _____ DATE _____

PAR _____ YARDAGE _____

SELF _____ SCORE _____ HANDICAP _____

PARTNER 1 _____ SCORE _____ HANDICAP _____

PARTNER 2 _____ SCORE _____ HANDICAP _____

PARTNER 3 _____ SCORE _____ HANDICAP _____

COMMENTS _____

_____

_____

Vichy Ses Sources travel poster.
Circa 1920. Artist unknown.
Wood River Gallery.

golf de Sarlabot
houlgate – cabourg

ROUNDS PLAYED

●

GOLF COURSE _____ DATE _____

PAR _____ YARDAGE _____

SELF _____ SCORE _____ HANDICAP _____

PARTNER 1 _____ SCORE _____ HANDICAP _____

PARTNER 2 _____ SCORE _____ HANDICAP _____

PARTNER 3 _____ SCORE _____ HANDICAP _____

COMMENTS _____

_____

_____

GOLF COURSE _____ DATE _____

PAR _____ YARDAGE _____

SELF _____ SCORE _____ HANDICAP _____

PARTNER 1 _____ SCORE _____ HANDICAP _____

PARTNER 2 _____ SCORE _____ HANDICAP _____

PARTNER 3 _____ SCORE _____ HANDICAP _____

COMMENTS _____

_____

_____

Golf de Sarlabot travel poster.
Circa 1935. Rene Vincent.
Wood River Gallery.

ROUNDS PLAYED

GOLF COURSE

DATE

PAR

YARDAGE

SELF

SCORE

HANDICAP

PARTNER 1

SCORE

HANDICAP

PARTNER 2

SCORE

HANDICAP

PARTNER 3

SCORE

HANDICAP

COMMENTS

GOLF COURSE

DATE

PAR

YARDAGE

SELF

SCORE

HANDICAP

PARTNER 1

SCORE

HANDICAP

PARTNER 2

SCORE

HANDICAP

PARTNER 3

SCORE

HANDICAP

COMMENTS

Biarritz Illustré. 1927. J. C. Haramboure. Laget Collection. Photo courtesy of Sally Fox, The Picture Company.

N° 6 (Nouvelle Série)   Le Numéro : 2 fr. 50   30 Septembre 1927

Biarritz Illustré
et Côte Basque Pyrénées

cette revue officielle est en lecture dans tous hotels, casinos, cercles, syndicats de la région, pyrénées côte basque, gascogne et dans le monde entier

J.C.Haramboure

LIST OF VISITORS   *Liste*   LISTA DE EXTRANJEROS
Officielle des Étrangers

publiée sous le haut patronage de la Fédération des Syndicats d'Initiative des pyrénées côte Basque et Gascogne

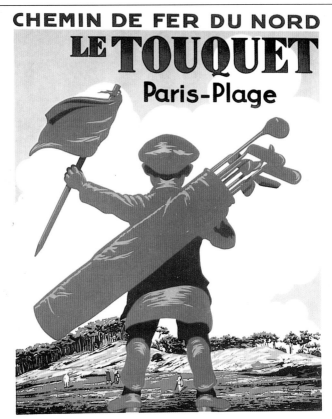

ROUNDS PLAYED

●

GOLF COURSE _____ DATE _____

PAR _____ YARDAGE _____

SELF _____ SCORE _____ HANDICAP _____

PARTNER 1 _____ SCORE _____ HANDICAP _____

PARTNER 2 _____ SCORE _____ HANDICAP _____

PARTNER 3 _____ SCORE _____ HANDICAP _____

COMMENTS _____

_____

_____

GOLF COURSE _____ DATE _____

PAR _____ YARDAGE _____

SELF _____ SCORE _____ HANDICAP _____

PARTNER 1 _____ SCORE _____ HANDICAP _____

PARTNER 2 _____ SCORE _____ HANDICAP _____

PARTNER 3 _____ SCORE _____ HANDICAP _____

COMMENTS _____

_____

_____

Le Touquet travel poster.
Circa 1930. Artist unknown.
Wood River Gallery.

69

●

ROUNDS PLAYED

●

GOLF COURSE _____   DATE _____

PAR _____   YARDAGE _____

SELF _____   SCORE _____   HANDICAP _____

PARTNER 1 _____   SCORE _____   HANDICAP _____

PARTNER 2 _____   SCORE _____   HANDICAP _____

PARTNER 3 _____   SCORE _____   HANDICAP _____

COMMENTS

_____

_____

GOLF COURSE _____   DATE _____

PAR _____   YARDAGE _____

SELF _____   SCORE _____   HANDICAP _____

PARTNER 1 _____   SCORE _____   HANDICAP _____

PARTNER 2 _____   SCORE _____   HANDICAP _____

PARTNER 3 _____   SCORE _____   HANDICAP _____

COMMENTS

_____

_____

●

Cannes travel poster. Artist unknown.
Wood River Gallery.

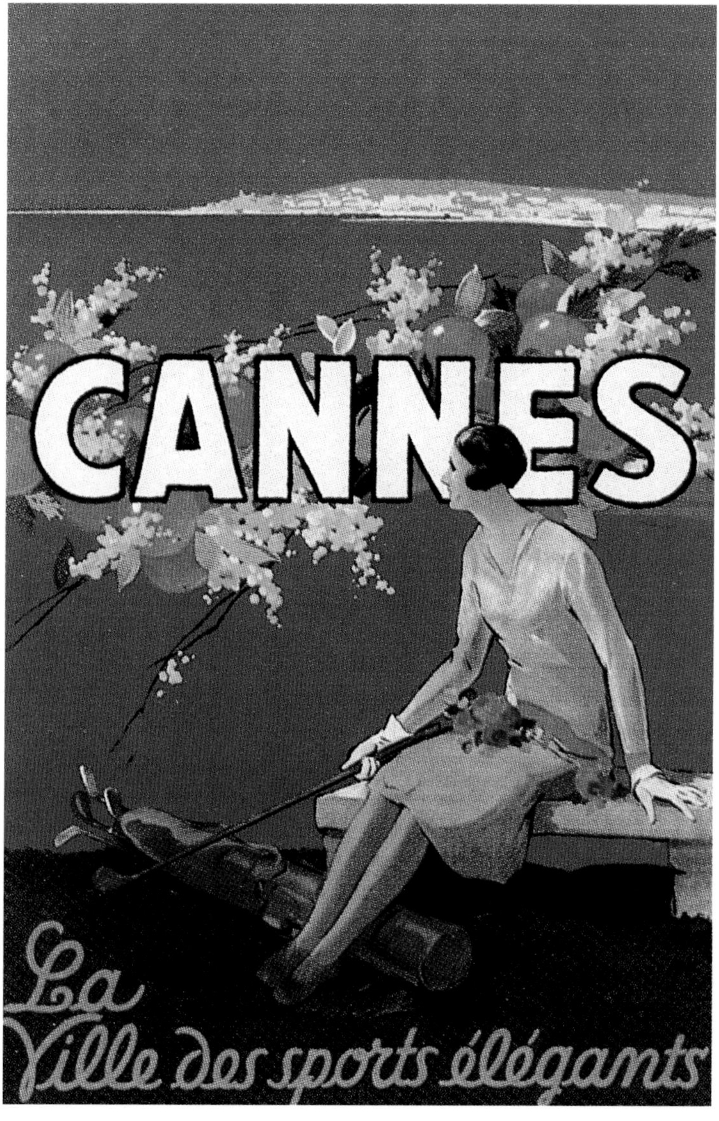
CANNES
La
Ville des sports élégants

THE KILLJOY

Price 15 cents

ROUNDS PLAYED

●

GOLF COURSE _____ DATE _____

PAR _____ YARDAGE _____

SELF _____ SCORE _____ HANDICAP _____

PARTNER 1 _____ SCORE _____ HANDICAP _____

PARTNER 2 _____ SCORE _____ HANDICAP _____

PARTNER 3 _____ SCORE _____ HANDICAP _____

COMMENTS _____

_____

_____

GOLF COURSE _____ DATE _____

PAR _____ YARDAGE _____

SELF _____ SCORE _____ HANDICAP _____

PARTNER 1 _____ SCORE _____ HANDICAP _____

PARTNER 2 _____ SCORE _____ HANDICAP _____

PARTNER 3 _____ SCORE _____ HANDICAP _____

COMMENTS _____

_____

_____

ROUNDS PLAYED

●

GOLF COURSE_____   DATE_____

PAR_____   YARDAGE_____

SELF_____   SCORE_____   HANDICAP_____

PARTNER 1_____   SCORE_____   HANDICAP_____

PARTNER 2_____   SCORE_____   HANDICAP_____

PARTNER 3_____   SCORE_____   HANDICAP_____

COMMENTS_____

_____

_____

GOLF COURSE_____   DATE_____

PAR_____   YARDAGE_____

SELF_____   SCORE_____   HANDICAP_____

PARTNER 1_____   SCORE_____   HANDICAP_____

PARTNER 2_____   SCORE_____   HANDICAP_____

PARTNER 3_____   SCORE_____   HANDICAP_____

COMMENTS_____

_____

_____

74
●

Liberty. September 28, 1940.
David Berger. Wood River Gallery.

SEPT. 28, 1940

Liberty

5¢

HOW JAPAN PLANS TO CONQUER AMERICA by Carl Crow

MURDER ON THE DIAMOND by Joe Medwick

"What should I take here, Caddie?"
"I should take a Guinness, Sir!"

ROUNDS PLAYED

●

GOLF COURSE _____ DATE _____

PAR _____ YARDAGE _____

SELF _____ SCORE _____ HANDICAP _____

PARTNER 1 _____ SCORE _____ HANDICAP _____

PARTNER 2 _____ SCORE _____ HANDICAP _____

PARTNER 3 _____ SCORE _____ HANDICAP _____

COMMENTS _____

_____

_____

GOLF COURSE _____ DATE _____

PAR _____ YARDAGE _____

SELF _____ SCORE _____ HANDICAP _____

PARTNER 1 _____ SCORE _____ HANDICAP _____

PARTNER 2 _____ SCORE _____ HANDICAP _____

PARTNER 3 _____ SCORE _____ HANDICAP _____

COMMENTS _____

_____

_____

John Bateman. Collection of Sarah
Fabian Baddiel, London.

●

ROUNDS PLAYED

●

GOLF COURSE _____ DATE _____

PAR _____ YARDAGE _____

SELF _____ SCORE _____ HANDICAP _____

PARTNER 1 _____ SCORE _____ HANDICAP _____

PARTNER 2 _____ SCORE _____ HANDICAP _____

PARTNER 3 _____ SCORE _____ HANDICAP _____

COMMENTS _____

_____

_____

GOLF COURSE _____ DATE _____

PAR _____ YARDAGE _____

SELF _____ SCORE _____ HANDICAP _____

PARTNER 1 _____ SCORE _____ HANDICAP _____

PARTNER 2 _____ SCORE _____ HANDICAP _____

PARTNER 3 _____ SCORE _____ HANDICAP _____

COMMENTS _____

_____

_____

●

Life. April 21, 1927. L. J. Holton.
Collection of Karen and Ralph Elder.

April 21 1927

Price 15 cents

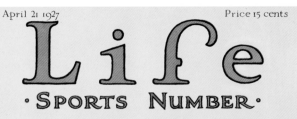

Life

· SPORTS NUMBER ·

The Sport of Missing Men

ROUNDS PLAYED

●

GOLF COURSE

DATE

PAR

YARDAGE

SELF

SCORE   HANDICAP

PARTNER 1

SCORE   HANDICAP

PARTNER 2

SCORE   HANDICAP

PARTNER 3

SCORE   HANDICAP

COMMENTS

GOLF COURSE

DATE

PAR

YARDAGE

SELF

SCORE   HANDICAP

PARTNER 1

SCORE   HANDICAP

PARTNER 2

SCORE   HANDICAP

PARTNER 3

SCORE   HANDICAP

COMMENTS

Life. July 24, 1931. Gilbert Bunch.
Collection of Karen and Ralph Elder.

81

●

ROUNDS PLAYED

●

GOLF COURSE _____ DATE _____

PAR _____ YARDAGE _____

SELF _____ SCORE _____ HANDICAP _____

PARTNER 1 _____ SCORE _____ HANDICAP _____

PARTNER 2 _____ SCORE _____ HANDICAP _____

PARTNER 3 _____ SCORE _____ HANDICAP _____

COMMENTS _____

_____

_____

GOLF COURSE _____ DATE _____

PAR _____ YARDAGE _____

SELF _____ SCORE _____ HANDICAP _____

PARTNER 1 _____ SCORE _____ HANDICAP _____

PARTNER 2 _____ SCORE _____ HANDICAP _____

PARTNER 3 _____ SCORE _____ HANDICAP _____

COMMENTS _____

_____

_____

82

●

GOLF COURSES

GOLF COURSE

ADDRESS

TEL

PAR

GREEN FEES

YARDAGE

COURSE DESIGNED BY

GOLF PRO

BOOKING RULES

COMMENTS

GOLF COURSE

ADDRESS

TEL

PAR

GREEN FEES

YARDAGE

COURSE DESIGNED BY

GOLF PRO

BOOKING RULES

COMMENTS

Southern California Union Pacific.
Artist unknown. Wood River Gallery.

85

GOLF COURSES

GOLF COURSE

ADDRESS

TEL   PAR

GREEN FEES   YARDAGE

COURSE DESIGNED BY

GOLF PRO

BOOKING RULES

COMMENTS

GOLF COURSE

ADDRESS

TEL   PAR

GREEN FEES   YARDAGE

COURSE DESIGNED BY

GOLF PRO

BOOKING RULES

COMMENTS

GOLF COURSES

GOLF COURSE

ADDRESS

TEL

PAR

GREEN FEES

YARDAGE

COURSE DESIGNED BY

GOLF PRO

BOOKING RULES

COMMENTS

GOLF COURSE

ADDRESS

TEL

PAR

GREEN FEES

YARDAGE

COURSE DESIGNED BY

GOLF PRO

BOOKING RULES

COMMENTS

GOLF COURSES

GOLF COURSE

ADDRESS

TEL

PAR

GREEN FEES

YARDAGE

COURSE DESIGNED BY

GOLF PRO

BOOKING RULES

COMMENTS

GOLF COURSE

ADDRESS

TEL

PAR

GREEN FEES

YARDAGE

COURSE DESIGNED BY

GOLF PRO

BOOKING RULES

COMMENTS

GOLF COURSES

GOLF COURSE

ADDRESS

TEL

PAR

GREEN FEES

YARDAGE

COURSE DESIGNED BY

GOLF PRO

BOOKING RULES

COMMENTS

GOLF COURSE

ADDRESS

TEL

PAR

GREEN FEES

YARDAGE

COURSE DESIGNED BY

GOLF PRO

BOOKING RULES

COMMENTS

GOLF COURSES

GOLF COURSE

ADDRESS

TEL

PAR

GREEN FEES

YARDAGE

COURSE DESIGNED BY

GOLF PRO

BOOKING RULES

COMMENTS

GOLF COURSE

ADDRESS

TEL

PAR

GREEN FEES

YARDAGE

COURSE DESIGNED BY

GOLF PRO

BOOKING RULES

COMMENTS

90

GOLF COURSES

GOLF COURSE

ADDRESS

TEL

PAR

GREEN FEES

YARDAGE

COURSE DESIGNED BY

GOLF PRO

BOOKING RULES

COMMENTS

GOLF COURSE

ADDRESS

TEL

PAR

GREEN FEES

YARDAGE

COURSE DESIGNED BY

GOLF PRO

BOOKING RULES

COMMENTS

GOLF COURSES

GOLF COURSE

ADDRESS

TEL

PAR

GREEN FEES

YARDAGE

COURSE DESIGNED BY

GOLF PRO

BOOKING RULES

COMMENTS

GOLF COURSE

ADDRESS

TEL

PAR

GREEN FEES

YARDAGE

COURSE DESIGNED BY

GOLF PRO

BOOKING RULES

COMMENTS

GOLF COURSES

GOLF COURSE

ADDRESS

TEL

PAR

GREEN FEES

YARDAGE

COURSE DESIGNED BY

GOLF PRO

BOOKING RULES

COMMENTS

GOLF COURSE

ADDRESS

TEL

PAR

GREEN FEES

YARDAGE

COURSE DESIGNED BY

GOLF PRO

BOOKING RULES

COMMENTS

Life

The Petting Green

GOLF PARTNERS

●

NAME

ADDRESS

HANDICAP

COMMENTS

TEL (H)   TEL (W)   FAX

NAME

ADDRESS

HANDICAP

COMMENTS

TEL (H)   TEL (W)   FAX

NAME

ADDRESS

HANDICAP

COMMENTS

TEL (H)   TEL (W)   FAX

Life. 1927. Artist unknown.
Wood River Gallery.

●

GOLF PARTNERS

●

NAME

ADDRESS

HANDICAP

COMMENTS

TEL (H)   TEL (W)   FAX

NAME

ADDRESS

HANDICAP

COMMENTS

TEL (H)   TEL (W)   FAX

NAME

ADDRESS

HANDICAP

COMMENTS

TEL (H)   TEL (W)   FAX

96

●

GOLF PARTNERS

●

NAME

ADDRESS

HANDICAP

COMMENTS

TEL (H)   TEL (W)   FAX

NAME

ADDRESS

HANDICAP

COMMENTS

TEL (H)   TEL (W)   FAX

NAME

ADDRESS

HANDICAP

COMMENTS

TEL (H)   TEL (W)   FAX

●

GOLF PARTNERS

NAME

ADDRESS

HANDICAP

COMMENTS

TEL (H)   TEL (W)   FAX

NAME

ADDRESS

HANDICAP

COMMENTS

TEL (H)   TEL (W)   FAX

NAME

ADDRESS

HANDICAP

COMMENTS

TEL (H)   TEL (W)   FAX

GOLF PARTNERS

NAME

ADDRESS

HANDICAP

COMMENTS

TEL (H)   TEL (W)   FAX

NAME

ADDRESS

HANDICAP

COMMENTS

TEL (H)   TEL (W)   FAX

NAME

ADDRESS

HANDICAP

COMMENTS

TEL (H)   TEL (W)   FAX

99

GOLF PARTNERS

NAME

ADDRESS

HANDICAP

COMMENTS

TEL (H)   TEL (W)   FAX

NAME

ADDRESS

HANDICAP

COMMENTS

TEL (H)   TEL (W)   FAX

NAME

ADDRESS

HANDICAP

COMMENTS

TEL (H)   TEL (W)   FAX

100

GOLF PARTNERS

NAME

ADDRESS

HANDICAP

COMMENTS

TEL (H)   TEL (W)   FAX

NAME

ADDRESS

HANDICAP

COMMENTS

TEL (H)   TEL (W)   FAX

NAME

ADDRESS

HANDICAP

COMMENTS

TEL (H)   TEL (W)   FAX

GOLF PARTNERS

●

NAME

ADDRESS

HANDICAP

COMMENTS

TEL (H)   TEL (W)   FAX

NAME

ADDRESS

HANDICAP

COMMENTS

TEL (H)   TEL (W)   FAX

NAME

ADDRESS

HANDICAP

COMMENTS

TEL (H)   TEL (W)   FAX

GOLF PARTNERS

NAME

ADDRESS

HANDICAP

COMMENTS

TEL (H)   TEL (W)   FAX

NAME

ADDRESS

HANDICAP

COMMENTS

TEL (H)   TEL (W)   FAX

NAME

ADDRESS

HANDICAP

COMMENTS

TEL (H)   TEL (W)   FAX

GOLF PARTNERS

NAME

ADDRESS

HANDICAP

COMMENTS

TEL (H)   TEL (W)   FAX

NAME

ADDRESS

HANDICAP

COMMENTS

TEL (H)   TEL (W)   FAX

NAME

ADDRESS

HANDICAP

COMMENTS

TEL (H)   TEL (W)   FAX

105

GOLF PARTNERS

●

NAME

ADDRESS

HANDICAP

COMMENTS

TEL (H)   TEL (W)   FAX

NAME

ADDRESS

HANDICAP

COMMENTS

TEL (H)   TEL (W)   FAX

NAME

ADDRESS

HANDICAP

COMMENTS

TEL (H)   TEL (W)   FAX

●

GOLF PARTNERS

NAME

ADDRESS

HANDICAP

COMMENTS

TEL (H)　　　　　　　　TEL (W)　　　　　　　　FAX

NAME

ADDRESS

HANDICAP

COMMENTS

TEL (H)　　　　　　　　TEL (W)　　　　　　　　FAX

NAME

ADDRESS

HANDICAP

COMMENTS

TEL (H)　　　　　　　　TEL (W)　　　　　　　　FAX

107

THE PRIVATE LIFE OF BARBARA STANWYCK

SEPT. 17, 1932

Liberty

5¢

America's Read Weekly

GOLF GAMES

There are many different ways to play golf — *play* in the sense of scoring and competing person against person, or team against team. In this section there are games that are designed for every conceivable level of player.

STROKE PLAY   The simplest and most common scoring method. The strokes taken on each hole are added together. The lowest score wins. The lowest score can be either gross or net depending on whether handicap is deducted.

FOUR BALL, BEST BALL   As above, except that each team of two players submits only the best score on each hole. Two advantages: a bad player doesn't drag down the team score, and speed. A player's ball can be picked up without the automatic loss of the hole.

FOURSOME: BEST BALL   All four players play together. The team records only the best score. This game encourages risk taking and aggressive play.

PINEHURST FOURSOMES   All four players drive. Each team selects the best drive, and the other member of the team then takes the next shot. Handicap by adding together the two players' individual handicaps, halving, and deducting from the gross score at the end of the round.

THROW OUT WORST HOLES   Decide before the game how many holes may be discarded — usually it is three. Add together the strokes taken on these holes and deduct from the total.

MATCH PLAY   The winner is the player who wins more *holes* than his opponent (although it is quite possible that he will have taken more *strokes*). Holes are either won, drawn or lost. Clearly it is not necessary to play a full nine or eighteen holes before a winner emerges.

FOUR BALL MATCH PLAY   Use the best score on each team to determine the winner of the hole. Handicap by deducting the lowest handicap of all four players from the other three players.

MATCH PLAY VERSUS PAR   Add the number of times that the player beats par and deduct those that are lost to par. The player with the most positive (or least negative) score wins.

Liberty. September 17, 1932.
Baldy McCowen. Wood River Gallery.

GOLF GAMES

BISQUE PAR COMPETITION Players get to deduct their handicap at will rather than as dictated on the scorecard. This enables better scores against par on difficult holes.

POINT COMPETITION The score at the end of each hole is rated by points, namely eight points for an eagle (two under par), six points for a birdie (one under par), four points for par and two points for bogey (one over par). All the above scores are net. Clearly, a disastrous hole will not have the same effect as in stroke play. It is also fast. If a player is not going to bogey, then the ball can be picked up.

STABLEFORD This is one of the basic — and oldest — forms of golf scoring. The scoring is four points for an eagle, three points for a birdie, two points for a par and one point for a bogey. Points are taken on net scores.

CLOSEST TO PIN/LONGEST DRIVE These two are very often used to add a little interest in tournaments. There needs to be a marker on which the name of the winning contestant (at any one point) can be written, and which will be placed on the spot where that ball has landed.

GREENIE The closest ball to the pin wins a point (or side bet). This is usually played on par-three holes.

ONE/TWO/THREE-CLUB COMPETITION This very challenging form of competition limits the golfer to playing the entire course with one, two or three clubs.

CALLAWAY Under the Callaway System, a player's handicap is determined after each round by deducting the worst individual scores a player makes during the first sixteen holes from the total eighteen holes. The table on page 111 shows the number of worst holes that may be deducted, as well as the adjustment. For instance, if the gross score for the eighteen holes is 96, the player turns to the table and opposite that score finds that he may deduct the total for his three worst holes scored on holes 1 through 16 inclusive. Thus, if he has one 9, one 8 and a 7, his handicap totals 24. From this total, a further plus or minus adjustment is made accordingly. (See adjustment at bottom of the table.)

GOLF GAMES

SCORE

					DEDUCT
—	—	70	71	72	Scratch—No adjustment
73	74	75	—	—	½ worst hole plus adjustment
76	77	78	79	80	1 " " " "
81	82	83	84	85	1½ " " " "
86	87	88	89	90	2 " " " "
91	92	93	94	95	2½ " " " "
96	97	98	99	100	3 " " " "
101	102	103	104	105	3½ " " " "
106	107	108	109	110	4 " " " "
111	112	113	114	115	4½ " " " "
116	117	118	119	120	5 " " " "
121	122	123	124	125	5½ " " " "
126	127	128	129	130	6 " " " "
131	132	133	134	135	6½ " " " "
136	137	138	139	140	7 " " " "

ADJUSTMENT

−2	−1	0	+1	+2	Add or adjust to handicap

Notes: 1. No hole must be scored at more than twice its par.   **2.** Half strokes count as whole.   **3.** Holes 17 and 18 are never deducted.   **4.** Maximum handicap is 50.   **5.** In case of ties, lowest handicap takes preference.

Golfer.
Collection of Sarah Fabian Baddiel, London.

Designed by Martine Bruel
Photo Research by Picture Research Consultants
Composition in Playboy by the Composing Room of New England
Futura, Futura Book, and Bold by Hamilton Phototype
Color separations, printing, and binding by Tien Wah Press Ltd.